Life Lessons

From The Man Who Listens To

Horses

A Field Guide to Inspire Your Own Journey

By Dr. Susan Cain and Debbie Roberts-Loucks with Monty Roberts

Table of Contents

Foreword

"Chronicling my life as the child of a brutal father, the process of writing brought me to the realization that not only did horses save me from his brutality, but they set me on a course to help make the world a better place for horses, and for people too."

- Monty Roberts

Very few people realize that Queen Elizabeth II, the Queen of England, requested I write my first book The Man Who Listens to Horses. I respected Her Majesty's wishes, but only reluctantly started to work on it. Pat and I had no computer, nor did we have any experience in producing a book. It's also true that the first publisher Her Majesty recommended said the book would sell between 3000 and 5000 copies and not even cover the cost of printing. This was very disappointing and led to plodding through six years in an attempt to produce a book the Queen and I could both view with pride.

Virtually every publisher in New York flatly turned down the manuscript. Random House London ultimately believed in the book, but wanted it to be called, The Man Who Talks to Horses. I strongly resisted, as I do not talk to horses. I communicate with them in their language. The book flew onto the English bestseller list, which prompted an immediate call from Random House New York. How crazy is that? Throughout my formal education, English was one of my weakest subjects. Once I began dating Pat, I had her do as much of the writing as she could. Words on paper were not my gig.

When Her Majesty first made the request, I remember asking, "Can't we just do another video?" With that the Queen suggested videos go away, but books are forever. I recall these conversations quite clearly and it is my memory the words from the Queen were stronger than a request. Her tone, her eyes, and her very words all said it was a demand. Don't for one moment think this was taken with any resentment. I was proud of Her Majesty's obvious interest, but scared to death of how in the world I was going to accomplish this with any degree of competence.

The following six years were punctuated by visits with the Queen where I offered various pages and received suggestions. The work was more like digging ditches than writing, but the outcome would positively impact my life, the lives of thousands of people, and millions of horses. It has been more than 6000 years since the domestication of these wonderful animals. During this time, the methods used to tame and train them changed very little. Violence, force, and demand were the centerpiece of virtually every training procedure horses were made to endure.

History tells us the early decades of training horses produced a mindset within their human counterparts that it was necessary to establish dominance through physical force. Generations came to believe it was absolutely essential. Many well-meaning trainers, including Xenaphon (240 B.C.) and Jeffries (early 1900's) tried to take the relationship in a more civilized direction, but it just didn't seem to work. Apparently, it was not until I came along with these crazy ideas about communication through gestures, producing one world champion after another, that accomplished horsemen began to see value in my concepts.

The Man Who Listens to Horses affected me in a very surprising way. Chronicling my life as the child of a brutal father, the process of writing brought me to the realization that not only did horses save me from his brutality, but they set me on a course to help make the world a better place for horses, and for people too. Going through the cathartic exercises necessary to call up the negative memories of my past, there was an entire redirection of my future. This book changed the course of my life in ways far more profound than simply causing me to be a less violent and a more successful horse trainer.

In addition to putting me on the road for 310 days out of each of the 16 years subsequent to its 1996 launch, the book's existence has driven me to every corner of the earth to help make the changes outlined on its pages. I believe it has significantly changed Her Majesty, the Queen and many of the people she depends upon in the training of horses in the Royal Stables. Thousands of people have told me this book has set them on a different course and improved their outlook toward dealing with animals of all kinds, while parents and teachers have praised its value for children.

There is probably no greater example of life changing than that of Michael Wood, a resident of Yorkshire, England. Michael recently gave an interview to the *Yorkshire Post*. The headline read: "The Book That Changed The Course Of My Life And Led To A Love Of Horses." Michael stated that many people have asserted a book changed the course of their lives. He went on to say that he doubts any one of them could mean it more than he did. Michael's article is filled with stories of his leaving a career to follow a course he took up because of the book.

Michael went on to state, "I can say, with hand on heart, that *The Man Who Listens to Horses* by Monty Roberts had a profound effect on the way I look at the world and live my life today. So profound, indeed, it inspired me to pack up a highly successful but unsatisfying career, rent out my house, buy some horses, and move to a garage that I was later to convert to a bungalow on the land that I bought for the horses." Following his dream, Michael is now founder and managing director of The Economy Radiator Company in Dalton, near Thirsk. Michael's story is one of tens of thousands that are quite similar.

The Man Who Listens to Horses has sold well past the five and one half million mark (est. 15 million readers) and is still selling today. Its impact has brought to me stories, not just about horses, but wives, children, families, prisoners, autistic individuals, and many other facets of life. The most recent area to consume much of my time is that of Post-Traumatic Stress Disorder. I am finding great results through my concepts for these heroes returning from combat with stress injuries that destroy lives and tear families apart. There has been a more rapid acceptance of the results of PTSD victims than there ever was from horse people.

Dog trainers, zookeepers, even people who handle cattle and other livestock have embraced the values of the concepts I've discovered. One should be ever mindful of the fact that I did not invent these principles, I only discovered they were already in place in nature and through circumstances that challenged my life, I was able to observe their value for animals and people. It is my opinion we will see a rapid ascent in the acceptance of these concepts, when brains far more brilliant than mine have the chance to process them and put them to work. I believe one will see vast improvement not only in the handling of horses, but all animals as well as the homes and schools of humans.

Queen Elizabeth II is the most unassuming person in a leadership role I have come to know in my entire career. The Queen is not likely to do it, but imagine how she would feel if she could step back and view the outcome of what was her idea, *The Man Who Listens to Horses.* Many world leaders become anxious to grab credit for almost any idea that passes by. Queen Elizabeth does not have this tendency even to the slightest degree. It is, however, my opinion that Queen Elizabeth II leads the world as the number one individual having had the strongest "influence" for good.

The Man Who Listens to Horses was clearly a learning experience for me. It brought out circumstances that had been lying dormant for decades, becoming a window through which I viewed a lifetime of being trained by a wonderful species called "Equus." My experience has been that a huge percentage of the readers were positively affected educationally and emotionally. Many experts have told me the learning curve of this book will continue for generations to come. If true, this book reaches out to the world as a tool for good far more profoundly than I could have ever dreamed.

What and who have influenced your journey? What have you fought for that has meaning and built purpose in your life? And how did you get there? This companion guide to my original book, *The Man Who Listens to Horses,* can help you revisit and capture your own compelling story. Your unique contribution to the world is profound and has the potential to affect untold numbers of others. I hope you enjoy this guide, and that it inspires your own journey.

- Monty Roberts | January 2013

Message from the Authors

I was standing with a group of students on Monty's front porch, watching him call wild deer with a peculiar whistle. They came, one by one, carefully eyeing the rest of us, striding confidently toward him. In a flash it occurred to me that here was the ultimate flight animal, and here was a person who has spent his life learning how to cultivate its trust. He had succeeded in decoding the silent language of flight animals. I wondered, what if his lessons could be applied outside of the equine realm? What value would there be in comparing the conditions of creating trust with a flight animal and a human "fight animal?" Pondering this, I became curious about how Monty's life could serve as a useful example to us all, so I followed his work as it crept outside of the bounds of the equine training world.

It came as no surprise that several years later, news arrived that Monty was now working with returning soldiers suffering from Post-Traumatic Stress Disorder. Broken, exposed to God-knows-what, unable to regain a foothold in their old lives, they came to Monty's farm. Their bewildered wives, husbands, or parents followed them, tentative and anxious. Each soldier was assigned a horse in the unlikely chance they could kindle some degree of mutual trust. And amazingly, they all did. They were taught "Equus," the non-verbal language of horses, how to Join-Up® with their horse, and how to earn and keep their respect. The tears and testimonies of these soldiers were proof that an emotional breakthrough had been achieved. Learning to hold accountability without force was a key lesson. "It's not post-traumatic stress disorder," Monty said summing up his work with veterans. "It's post-traumatic stress injury."

In June 2011, Queen Elizabeth II honored Monty by making him a member of the Royal Victorian Order. She not only endorsed his work, but also sealed his fate as the trusted source of excellence in equine training methods worldwide. Instead of 15 minutes of fame, Monty has increased his success by staying true to his mission statement: "To leave the world a better place for horses and for people, too." He has helped humans repair their lives when violence has intervened. He has fostered 47 children, trained countless numbers of people in his methods, and enlightened scores of readers who have benefited from *The Man Who Listens to Horses*. Monty has appeared on television, radio, in movies, and even on the London stage where he assisted with the production of War Horse. He has authored numerous columns and books, which have been translated into many languages. His work has reached far beyond the equine world to touch millions of lives.

Yet Monty does not play the part of a privileged celebrity. He has dined with everyone from sheiks and monarchs, to meth addicts and the homeless. He is a real person, capable of blasting away at students when they fail to live up to his expectations, correcting them with a terse remark. But he is also loved by his students. Many attest he is a fair judge, offering the same consequences to humans that he offers to horses by employing his use of "instant positive and instant negative" consequences. The trust-based approach he uses allows Monty to level with his students without dominating them, the same skill required of effective leaders in today's workplace. Monty often stresses, "I don't want students to be as good as I am; I want them all to be a lot better."

Those unfamiliar with Monty's early discovery of the language of horses often brand him as an imitator of the very methods he discovered. But his initial discoveries have served as the foundation for what the industry now calls "natural horsemanship." Leaders pay a high price for their willingness to be public figures, and Monty is no exception. The fact remains this American cowboy, who came from nowhere to offer an alternative to violence for animals and humans, has in fact succeeded far beyond his own expectations. How can we learn from his life's lessons?

Monty's life and work are featured as a case study in this book. You will discover how he persisted in his early years, when faced with discouragement and disbelievers. You will read about how Monty responded to business setbacks as his career developed, how he leveraged the "luck" he encountered, and how his persistence paid off. We've spent a year digging into Monty's work from every angle. The fascinating information we found and feedback we received will inspire you and draw you closer to wanting to capitalize on your own passions and potential.

This book serves as a field guide to spark your journey. With respect and awe for those of you who follow your passion down to launching and sustaining a successful business, we offer this book as a way to learn vital business lessons from *The Man Who Listens to Horses*.

- **Susan Cain, Ed D. | September 2012**

In 1989, the Thoroughbred racing industry was in bad financial shape, and Monty's business was suffering. He and his wife Pat (my parents) had spent the previous 20 years investing in their successful careers as bloodstock agents and world class developers of young race horses. In fact, for 19 of those years, they had been the leading consigners of the two-year olds in training sales in the United States. Some of their young protégés hold titles such as Horse of the World and twice winner of the L'Arc de Triomphe. This attracted the attention of one of the greatest collectors of quality thoroughbred racehorses in the world at the time: the Queen of England.

Since 1980, profits had been plummeting at American racetracks. As a result, money was being diverted to developing state lottery systems and the growing Indian gambling casinos. It was clear the industry was changing, but the racing world was blind to the need for reaching out to a younger audience. As a sport, racing wasn't as attractive as it had been and gambling was becoming more accessible than simply going to the track to bet. Training horses was rapidly becoming a shrinking service industry. When Monty received the call from Her Majesty, it seemed like an opportunity to expand his training of race horses, but that never manifested.

Instead, Queen Elizabeth endorsed his work, put him on the road to train her horse trainers, and insisted he write a book. The publisher she recommended told Monty it would sell three to four thousand copies. And it did… on the first day. *The Man Who Listens to Horses* went on to become a New York Times bestseller and spent 58 weeks on the list. Monty was now beginning a new career at age 61.

We hope this companion piece will help you to recognize and believe there are many opportunities you can create if you work diligently to uncover them. If Monty had not developed these qualities, we would not have the opportunity to enjoy the inspiring stories in *The Man Who Listens to Horses*.

- Debbie Roberts-Loucks | December 2012

Introduction
About this Field Guide

"Writing a book is an adventure. To begin with it is a toy and an amusement. Then it becomes a mistress, then it becomes a master, then it becomes a tyrant. The last phase is that just as you are about to be reconciled to your servitude, you kill the monster and fling him to the public."

- Winston Churchill

What you are holding in your hands is a lifetime of lessons from Monty Roberts. We have combed through Monty's life; his writings and interviews. We have surveyed and talked with people all over the world who have been impacted by his work. We taught a doctoral class on his methods, transferring them to the workplace to see how they would benefit personal and organizational development. We're glad you're here and we are ready for you.

Monty Roberts' story will take you from his early days on the dusty rodeo circuit and the sweeping vistas of the Santa Ynez Valley, to the great palaces of England. We got very curious about his path. How did he build an international business, a working horse farm, and a sustainable non-profit organization? What lessons can we learn from his experiences? What qualities allowed him to successfully ride his career rollercoaster, and what role did the social context at time contribute to his setbacks and success?

This field guide was a challenge to write. Monty has, through the years, created so many lessons that it was hard to narrow our focus. What we have done is to focus on key lessons we hope will resonate with you.

Download a paper copy of the Life Lessons Toolkit to use at:
http://corplearning.com/life-lessons_resources.html

Post comments about your own journey ahead on our Facebook page at:
https://www.facebook.com/LifeLessonsFromTheManWhoListensToHorses?ref=hl

How to use this Field Guide

The field guide follows the book, *The Man Who Listens to Horses, The Story of a Real-Life Horse Whisperer*. It is truly a companion book. Each of the eight lessons corresponds to a chapter in the book. We have chosen stories from each chapter to focus on core lessons in living. The lessons are listed in reading order as they appear in the book, allowing you to read both at the same time, if you choose. You may notice we have edited some stories so they fit within the context of a learning lesson format.

We have left many other excellent stories and anecdotes out, although these deserve a thorough reading as well. Monty's life story continues beyond the confines of his original book and this field guide. Find out more about what he is currently up to at www.montyroberts.com. We hope you enjoy the selection we've created -- and that their lessons serve you well.

NOTE: Users of the eBook, please follow along with the "Life Lessons" pages on your own separate sheet of paper to make maximum use of each lesson!

Special Thanks...

To Debi Giese of Mode Design for the great graphics, (debi@modedesignco.com), Tim Buividas, Ron Skubisz and Ben Knerr from the Corporate Learning Institute for putting it all together, Connie Cain and Melissa Ericksen for your editing inputs. Thanks for all that you have done.

eBook formatting by Ben Knerr at bknerr@corplearning.com

Book Design by Mode Design, www.modedesignco.com

Spot Light on Join-Up

Debbie Roberts-Loucks Interviews Monty Roberts on the Gift of Join-Up:

Debbie Roberts-Loucks has been with Monty and Pat Roberts Inc. since 2002. She is also their eldest daughter. She recently took time to delve deeper into the Join-Up process by interviewing her father.

Debbie: Can you define Join-Up?

Monty: Join-Up is a process by which a human utilizes a combination of predator and equine signals (typically those of the lead mare in a herd) to propose a relationship of cooperation in which the human will take the decision makers position (just as the lead mare in a herd does). This process is complete when a horse chooses to be with a human rather than away from him. Horses have survived for millions of years, avoiding predators by being ever wary of their environment and only giving their trust to those who have earned it. A horse's first instinct is to take flight from anything they are not familiar with. Imagine the first time a horse meets a human who understands the horse's gestures of communication and "communicates" with them.

Debbie: As a teenager, you discovered that horses have a silent communication system based on gestures. You've spent your lifetime studying and teaching others to communicate with a horse in what you call "Equus." Can you tell us more about this?

Monty: These signals are non-verbal, predictable, discernible, and effective. The elements are really quite simple, but simplicity becomes their greatest strength.

Debbie: Join-Up is the gift you developed for the rest of us who needed a process to understand how to communicate with the horse, in order to create an environment of cooperation. What prompted you to do this?

Monty: I first developed Join-Up to stop the cycle of violence typically used in traditional horse breaking. Through a process of clear communication and mutual trust, horses are motivated to be willing partners as they accept the first saddle, bridle, and rider of their life in less than thirty minutes.

Debbie: Join-Up evolved into a process based upon communication to create a bond rooted in trust. How does it achieve this?

Monty: It must be nonviolent and can only be accomplished if both partners are relaxed at the end of the process. To gain Join-Up with a horse, it is necessary to step into his world, observe his needs, conditions, and the rules that govern his social order. One should learn to communicate in Equus, since we know he cannot communicate in our verbal language. This process cannot be faked. Once understood, it is easy to use and can be trust-building for both human and horse.

Debbie: So Join-Up is a tool with which to create a safe and comfortable environment for ongoing communication. Can anyone learn to do this?

Monty: The tool must be used with skill, which may take years to perfect, but in its basic form can be learned quickly. Join-Up works at any stage during this partnership between man and horse, whether it is a new one or one of long standing. Join-Up between human and horse heralds an end to isolation and separation of both our species by bonding through communication. It is a procedure that should be precisely followed; there are no short cuts. Join-Up may bring out conflict and perceived resistance or even ambivalence. However, if the trainer is competent, believes in the concept, and executes it reasonably well, the horse will respond positively. It is imperative that anyone employing Join-Up is fully responsible for their own actions.

Debbie: Since violence must have no part in the process of Join-Up, how can you ensure the horse will respond the way you hope?

Monty: Violence of any kind will destroy the effectiveness of the procedure. A trainer must move through the process keeping the conversation alive, always allowing the horse time to respond. Join-Up is response-based, not demand-based. The trainer should comply with two significant conceptual rules:

  1. Time is not the important thing! Good horses are! An equine partner of the highest caliber should be the goal. A trainer should enter the process of Join-Up with the idea that time is not limited. This attitude will maximize results in the minimum amount of time. Horses are animals of synchronicity. If the trainer's heart rate or adrenaline increases, the horse will sync with this physiology. I say, adrenaline up; learning down. Adrenaline down; learning up.

  2. The second most important point to remember is that the trainer waits for the horse to do something right and rewards him. He does not wait for the horse to do something wrong and punish him.

The Following Tools Are Used Within the Context of This Field Guide

Personal Strengths Shield

Personal Resilience Checklist

Trust-Based Communication Model

Steps to Defining Your Core Values

Personal Gifts Inventory

Personal Development Plan

Download the toolkit at <u>http://corplearning.com/life-lessons_resources.html</u>

LESSON 1

Value Your Purpose

"I had chanced on something important but could not know it would shape my life…"

- Monty Roberts

Wild Mustangs graze on the High Sierra Plains

"The vision that you glorify in your mind, the ideal that you enthrone in your heart, this you will build your life by, and this you will become."

- Anonymous

We know from the Acknowledgments in *The Man Who Listens to Horses* that the book serves as a kind of flashback. We enter Monty Robert's life at age 54, as he is ushered into a new career as the Queen of England's trusted trainer. How did he get there, and what was the road like on the way? In Chapter One, *The Call of the Wild Horses*, Monty startles us with his keen sense of adventure and shocking sensibilities for one so young. There we are, with Monty in the High Sierra Desert, lying on our bellies, as the warm desert wind whips past us. And there are the Mustangs -- now standing, now running, now quiet, now nipping and restless. Monty's first teachers were horses, and from his early perspective, we learn how these teachers set the stage for his developing sense of purpose.

Monty Discovers a Meaningful Connection

While tracking wild Mustangs in Nevada as a boy, Monty Roberts observed a kind of communication between the horses, a silent language he would later call "Equus." Monty has incorporated "Equus" into his nonviolent training approach. One of his earliest discoveries was the adoption of a gentling process for untamed horses he calls Join-Up. Monty first developed Join-Up to stop the cycle of violence typically used in traditional horse breaking. Convinced there must be a more effective yet gentle method, Monty used the horse's inherent methods of communication and herd behavior to develop mutual trust. The result is a willing partnership in which the horse's performance can flourish to its full potential, rather than exist within the boundaries of obedience. Without the use of pain or force, the trainer persuades a raw and untamed horse to accept a saddle, bridle, and rider in less than 30 minutes. To see how Monty accomplishes this:

Watch a Join-Up on YouTube: "Monty Roberts Join Up Example" (http://www.montyroberts.com/contacts/videos/)

Monty's Vision and Purpose Began Early in His Life

CASE STUDY: *Monty's vision for developing an alternative training method began to take shape while he was very young:*

I had come to think of my process as entirely different from that of 'breaking' horses. The word 'breaking' has connotations of violence and domination, and damage done to the object concerned. I changed the nomenclature. I called my method 'starting' horses. My aim was to head in the opposite direction from the 'sacking out' procedure. If sacking out was designed to cause fear in the horse, then I wanted the opposite. I wanted to create trust.

QUESTIONS TO PONDER

- What about you? What early experiences shaped your values and perspective?

- Did they help develop your sense of personal vision or purpose?

THE POWER OF PURPOSE

In his book, *Drive, The Surprising Truth about What Motivates Us*, author Dan Pink sifts through the current research on motivation. What he finds is that extrinsic rewards -- he calls them "if-then" rewards -- work for certain short-term tasks, but long-lasting personal motivation comes from three sources: autonomy, mastery, and purpose. Together, these three motivators drive individuals to perform at their best. Pink shares a story about the Atlasian Company, where employees are given an opportunity to work on projects that interested them on company time. The result was a spike in innovation and product development. Given the opportunity, most of us will seek personal challenges that have meaning to us, allowing us to work on our own toward mastery. In the round pen, Monty sets the course for learning by allowing the horse to make his own autonomous decisions. Monty says, "no one has the right to say you must, or I will hurt you." The horse is free to choose to join up or not, and masters the situation by deciding to join the human in what turns out to be an excellent purpose -- an escape from fear toward a trusting relationship.

Looking deeper into your sense of purpose can be a useful tool for increasing motivation, by reviewing your strengths and creating a working definition of what you find important and valuable. In this lesson, we have created a kind of blueprint, what we call your Personal Strengths Shield. It encompasses what you find valuable, what fills you with positive energy and fuels your efforts.

Knowing what you value and how you are intrinsically motivated allows you to sustain momentum and inspiration, despite the challenges you will undoubtedly face.

CASE STUDY: *The Gift of Vision- Is it Worth the Price?*

The story of Monty's discovery and development of Equus and Join-Up offers a fascinating glimpse into the challenges he encountered while developing his personal vision for the future.

And as it happened, I discovered something so exciting I began to be sure that I could persuade even my father to see things my way. I'd identified a phenomenon which I called "Join-Up." As I lay in bed at night I could hardly sleep, I was so convinced I had stumbled on something which would change the way we operated with horses. It was 100 percent proof, as far as I was concerned, that I was on the right track, that the efforts I was making were worthwhile. I was so excited by it, and so sure of it, given what I had accomplished in the concentrated atmosphere generated by having to start so many horses in a short time, that I knew my father would latch on to it as well. He was too experienced a horseman not to.

However, after what had happened before, I wasn't going to go and show him directly. Instead, I settled on showing Ray Hackworth, in the sure knowledge that Ray could prevail over my father because he had his respect. Ray Hackworth was a noted trainer and a gentleman: soft-spoken, but also a disciplinarian. I asked him to come and watch what I could do. I told him I had discovered a new phenomenon which I could explain only in terms of the horse's own language. I promised him it was true, that I could dissolve the natural barrier between horse and man, flight animal and fight animal.

He reminded me that my father had often warned me that my ideas could be dangerous and I should stick to the conventional ways of doing things. But I continued to ask him to come and watch what I could do. I was certain I could impress him enough to talk to my father in a positive way about what he was about to see.

Eventually he agreed to come and watch. When we arrived at the round pen, Ray strolled up the ramp on to the viewing deck and positioned himself leaning against the fence. "OK," he said, tipping his hat to the back of his head. "Go ahead. Let's see it."

From practicing this a hundred times over, I knew what to do. I had developed a confidence in my attitude. I waited a moment or two to allow this un-named, perfectly wild Mustang to become accustomed to the round pen. He was too nervous to take a single step towards me, although his attention was on me as the main threat currently confronting him. "What I'm going to do," I said to Ray, "is kind of use the same language as the dominant mare in his family group." There was silence from Ray up on the viewing deck, so I figured I was there to explain myself and I'd better get on with it. He wasn't going to stop and ask questions.

"And that language is a silent language, a body language," I continued, "and the first thing I'm going to ask him to do is to go away from me, to flee. I'm only doing this because then I want to ask him to come back and Join-Up with me."

Monty continued his work with the colt until a Join-Up was completed. He then explained the next steps to Ray Hackworth.

Now I had the colt walking comfortably behind me and I knew Ray Hackworth would be amazed, watching from the viewing gallery above the fence. I imagined him telling my father how much I had accomplished "I tell you, Marvin, that boy of yours had a wild horse walking along behind him like it was his best friend after about 15 minutes. He's on to something. Come down and see for yourself," he'd say.

Then my father would walk over with Ray Hackworth and ask what all this was about. I couldn't help predicting his amazement. I called out to Ray – as quietly as possible now the colt was standing next to me - "Ray, you know, now that he's joined up with me and we're on the same side, it's pretty much of a formality."

Ray Hackworth's silhouette was immobile, and with the late afternoon sun slanting in from that side of the round pen, I couldn't read his expression. I called out, "We're thirty minutes into the starting procedure, now." Although I was talking to him, I didn't dare glance at Ray. I felt his eyes on me, and I knew he could not fail to be impressed at what he was seeing. I said to Ray, "I want to gain his confidence and make him happy to follow the bit and bridle -- as he'll be doing just that for the rest of his working life. I want to make it a happy experience for him."

Within 30 minutes, Monty had a saddle and bridle on the willing colt and was riding him.

Looking up at Ray Hackworth, who was staring at me with a concerned look on his face, I was sure he realized what an incredible discovery I'd made, and that subsequently my father's opinion could be turned around by this man whom he regarded as his equal. I was an idealistic child of 14 and, as I sat there in triumph on the back of this horse, I believed it was only a matter of a few weeks before I would be enjoying the respect and admiration of my elders and betters all over the county. Instead, from his position on the viewing platform, Ray barked out, "That was a fluke!"

The sound of his voice coincided with the colt's first steps and I didn't try to stop him. We just walked around together while Ray continued calling out to me, "You're very wrong to go against your father's advice. If I were you, I'd cease messing around like this; it could end up with you lying seriously injured in the middle of that round pen there. I wouldn't like to predict what the injury will be, but for a start you'll be trampled or kicked, even before you get to be bucked off."

He continued in this vein as he walked from the viewing deck and disappeared from sight. I could still hear him making disparaging remarks as he went across the yard to the barns he leased from the Competition Grounds, which were adjacent to mine. I was left riding the colt around, crushed by disappointment at the very moment when I should have been triumphant. The people whose respect and guidance I needed were refusing to give it.

I vowed never to mention my ideas to anyone again.

QUESTIONS TO PONDER

- Monty encountered a crippling blow to his sense of purpose and personal vision. Has this ever happened to you?

- In what ways can a personal sense of your strengths, values, or purpose help you rebound from disappointments?

LEARNING TOOL
Personal Strengths Shield–
Your Weapon against Self-Doubt

The Johari Window model is a simple format, which was devised by Joseph Luft and Harry Ingham. The window is actually a drawing of four squares and helps you develop awareness of your self-perception, as well as how others perceive you. The four windows include information about you (that you and everyone knows), things you hide about yourself; things you are blind to but others know; and an area called "the unknown" that represents potential growth and personal insights. We have adapted this model for you to use below. Enjoy creating your personal strengths shield. It serves as a blueprint for identifying your strengths. Without over-thinking, try to capture and write down the following:

SPACE 1: Open Information: Record the strengths you know you have, as well as those you are known for.

SPACE 2: Blind Information: Record the strengths you do not know about. This will require you to ask others how they see your strong points.

SPACE 3: Hidden Information: Record the strengths you are hiding from the world. Like Monty, when he decided to hide his Join-Up technique, what strengths, abilities, convictions, and achievements have you hidden or "disowned?"

SPACE 4: Unknown: This area represents the potential growth you could make by exploring, risking, and pushing past those self-imposed limitations. Record what you would dare to do, if you could.

Personal Strengths Shield

Open Information:
Place strengths here that you know you have and that you are known for.

Blind Information:
Place strengths here that you do not yet know about-this one will require you to go ask others how they see your strong points and strengths.

Hidden Information:
What strengths are you protecting or hiding from the world?

Unknown:
This area represents the potential growth you could achieve by exploring, risking, and pushing past self-imposed limitations. What would you dare to do if you *could?*

Your Personal Strengths Shield

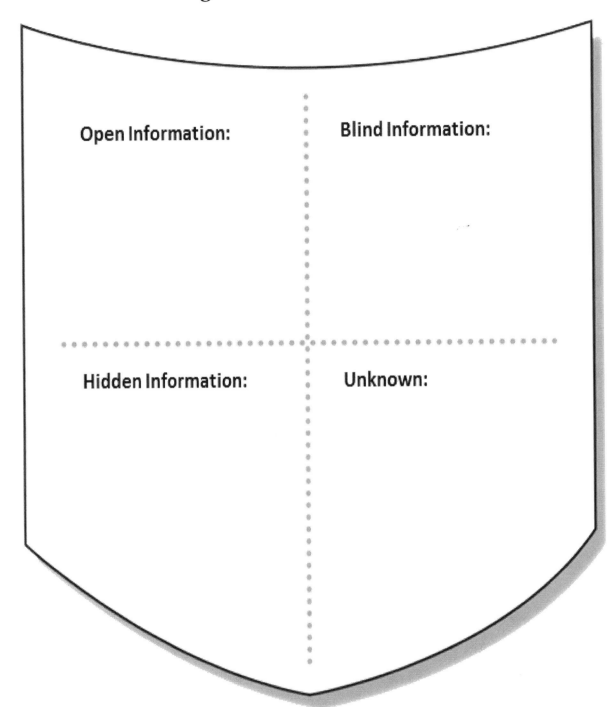

Open Information:

Blind Information:

Hidden Information:

Unknown:

LESSON ONE TAKE-AWAYS

- Knowing and valuing your strengths can act as a shield against self-doubt.

- Taking risks leads to increased learning.

- Awareness and appreciation of your own unique strengths and values can help you rebound from disappointments.

- It is easy to give up when others do not affirm you. Persistence takes courage and a deeper belief in your purpose and vision.

Notes:

"My goal is to leave the world a better place than I found it, for horses and people too."

- Monty Roberts

LESSON 2

Adversity - The Launch Pad for Personal Inspiration & Innovation

"I was born at a time when the world was still mired in the woes of the Great Depression."

-Monty Roberts

In Chapter Two, *Growing Up With Horses*, Monty takes us through his developing years with horses; through the adversarial relationship he endured with his father, towards the formative years that inspired him and shaped his creative muscle.

Monty on Ginger, his trusted companion and equine "babysitter"

The Value of Adversity

"The most beautiful people we have known are those who have known defeat, known suffering, known struggle, known loss, and have found their way out of the depths. These persons have an appreciation, sensitivity, and an understanding of life that fills them with compassion, gentleness, and a deep loving concern. Beautiful people do not just happen."

- **Elisabeth Kübler-Ross**

What adversity have you experienced in your life? How has it informed you?

In Chapter Two, *Growing Up With Horses*, you can read about Monty's early life and the uncertainties his parents faced during the time of the Second World War. Like Monty and his parents, the present economy has shredded our confidence in economic certainties. For those old enough to know that economic certainty has never really existed in the first place, that may be a very good thing. Adversity is a teacher to us all.

Monty Roberts was born during the Great Depression, in May 1935, when the only economic certainty was that people would be poor. Here he got his start as a talented young rider, helping to earn a living for this family. Adversity came early, not just because Monty was born in difficult economic times, but because of his father's brutality.

CASE STUDY: *Early adversity- How an adverse relationship sparked Monty's sense of compassion*

Monty's parents managed several income streams during his youth, including riding stables, horse training operations, and prize money from Monty's rodeo competition days. Although Monty's relationship with his mother was close, his father's directive and punitive training methods alienated him. Monty recalls his early life with his father this way:

Everything I have achieved has come to me because of the early and concentrated exposure to horses that (my father) gave me. At the same time, if my professional life can be described as having a direction, it is facing away from him. The vigor with which I have pursued that direction is a consequence of my outright rebellion against (my father) and his methods.

My father was a tall man of a slim, muscular build, with chiseled features under light brown hair. He was as neat and orderly as circumstances allowed. If he met a fraternal friend in the town, I'd say he could be a friendly, inviting man. However, from the outset he turned a cold and critical eye on me. He was unforgiving and scrutinized everything I did, more often than not holding it up to ridicule. His methods of dealing with horses were what I would describe as conventional -- that is to say, cruel.

QUESTIONS TO PONDER

- In what way was Monty's father instrumental in the development of Monty's values and concepts?

- In your own life, who has played a key role in your struggle to develop your values and beliefs?

_____

_____

_____

_____

_____

_____

_____

_____

_____

_____

_____

_____

"It is interesting to notice how some minds seem almost to create themselves, springing up under every disadvantage, and working their solitary but irresistible way through a thousand obstacles."

- **Washington Irving**

Monty built a career that went in the opposing direction of his father's. He was against his father's approach to training horses, as well as his treatment of people. This reaction fueled Monty's interest in finding common sense alternatives that offered more compassion.

How Adversity Informs Leaders Later In Life

How does adversity affect your personal development? A study done on high profile leaders by H.E. Haller (2005) found that while many leaders viewed adversity experienced early in life as important, they did not identify it as the most important or seminal event in their lives. Haller found that leaders saw obstacles and adversity as challenges which could be turned into opportunities.

They felt that facing adversity and successfully overcoming obstacles was important in their growth. The study also found that having mentors to help guide a leader's life, motivating and inspiring them was essential. These early experiences led many leaders to adopt a kind of Servant-Leadership Style, serving others through selflessness and humility. Many of these leaders also reported that having religious or relationship ties was essential in overcoming obstacles. Perhaps Haller's most powerful contribution is to make clear that the value of early adversity is to act as a catalyst for later leadership development.

Coping Skills that Help Overcome Adversity

Individual resilience is a person's ability to positively cope with stressors and setbacks. Developing resilience is learning process. Several studies have focused on the development of resilience in reaction to setbacks. Researchers Aguirre (2007) and Bonanno (2004) have found that resilience is more commonplace than extraordinary, and that people everywhere regularly demonstrate resiliency. They also found that:

- Resilience is not a trait people either have or do not have.

- Resilience involves behaviors, thoughts, and actions that can be learned and developed in anyone.

- Resilience is tremendously influenced by a person's environment.

Research supports that people can build resilience and create a resilient foundation anytime in life. Monty rebounded from his own setbacks by believing in his convictions, being honest and authentic about his beliefs, and taking risks based on his core values.

LEARNING TOOL
Increasing your Resilience Levels

Take a moment to look through the following checklist of traits that nurture resilience. **Check the ones** that you feel you already do well. Then think about how you might be able to use these strengths even more. For the traits you did not check, how can you begin to develop strengths in these areas as well?

PERSONAL RESILIENCE LEVELS

- ○ *Making connections with others*
- ○ *Looking for opportunities for self-discovery*
- ○ *Nurturing a positive view of self*
- ○ *Accepting that change is a part of living*
- ○ *Taking decisive actions*
- ○ *Learning from the past*

One of the critical factors that boost resilience are the relationships that foster affirmation in your life. Monty shares a story about one person in particular that made a difference to his early resilience levels:

CASE STUDY: *Relationships that Make a Difference*

Marguerite Parsons was a figure of central importance in my life. She had been our nanny since I was two or three years old, and now she became my teacher as well. Neat, clean and as steady as a rock, she read me stories and made learning fun. Above all, she was instructive.

She understood me better than my parents did and sympathized with my problems. She not only taught me how to communicate with people but also encouraged me to relax, and to understand that if I was to pursue a career as a horseman with such single-minded dedication from such a young age, I would have to pace myself in order not to burn out.

QUESTIONS TO PONDER

- Monty received affirmation from his relationships with horses and people. Do you have central figures in your life -- human or otherwise -- who have given you support and recognition? Who are they?

- Does cultivating a support network help you cope with adversity? How can you expand your support network?

- How has the adversity in your life impacted your personal motivation, and how can it continue to inform your direction?

LESSON TWO TAKE-AWAYS

- Adversity is important for shaping potential as well as compassion.

- Many leaders report that adversity has helped them develop effective life and leadership skills.

- Resilience is an important protectant against stress in your life. Since research shows that resilience is learned, you too can improve your resilience levels.

- Key relationships help fuel self-worth and serve as a protectant support factor.

Notes:

"If I can help people learn that violence is not the answer, how gratifying that is and how incredible."

- Monty Roberts

LESSON 3

Rebounding from Adversity
Using Authentic Communication & Risk

"I never really had a childhood."

-Monty Roberts

In Chapter Three, *East of Eden*, we watch Monty struggle through his days on the rodeo circuit toward his early career years. It's a slippery uphill climb, as he takes on each new challenge that presents itself and rebounds from setbacks along the way.

Monty completing a successful Join-Up. (Left). Monty signing copies of his book. (Right)

Setbacks as Opportunity

"It was high counsel that I once heard given to a young person: always do what you are afraid to do."

- Ralph Waldo Emerson

Monty learned from failures as well as from successes. Despite these setbacks and also because of them, Monty rose to the top of his field as a respected icon. How did he do it? What lessons do they offer you?

Using an Authentic Communication Approach

In his life, Monty has had to defend his training approach countless times, but in doing so has rarely been *defensive*. Instead, he uses a naturally authentic communication style that has allowed him to deliver his message in a non-judgmental and concise way. Monty uses the same authentic approach with horses to foster mutual trust and respect. Think of authentic communication as being the way you converse with someone when you believe in your message so much it needs no defense. Author Susan Scott, whose book *Fierce Conversations* teaches the value of authentic conversation, suggests "Come out from behind yourself and make the conversation real." In her view, honest communication builds trusting relationships.

In the round pen, Monty approaches horses using a conversation based on trust and respect. He calls this approach *trust-based communication*. Once horses discover that the trainer is trustworthy, they can commit to a relationship rather than complying out of fear. Just remember, it isn't easy to apply this approach to relationships -- human or animal. Building trust instead of using force takes more time, more patience, and more caring. This isn't the as same as just being nice to someone. Building trust involves trial and error learning. Building trust involves clear, non-defensive communication. As Susan Scott notes, trust is built "...one conversation at a time."

CASE STUDY: *The Lasting Impact of Authentic Communication*

Monty once had a teacher who challenged him in an unusual way:

Mr. Fowler paced back and forth at the head of the class, while we students waited with our pencils sharpened and our paper at the ready. A tall man with an erect bearing and an olive complexion, he always dressed immaculately.

"I want you all to think about this very carefully," said Mr. Fowler, waving his long, elegant hands. "It should be like painting a picture of your lives in the future, as if all your ambitions had been realized."

A voice piped up. "How much detail d'you want, sir?"

"As much as possible. It should be a complete portrayal of what you envision for yourselves in the future." He turned to gaze at us calmly." And my last instruction to you is perhaps the most important: this vision of the future that you're all going to paint for me should be a realistic one. I don't want to hear about some crazy, off-the-wall plan. I don't want to know about any Hollywood dreams, either."

There was a smattering of laughter at this idea. We were in California, after all. He finished by saying, "It should be a fair and accurate assessment of where I might expect to find you if I were to visit you in your mid-thirties. It's to be called "My Goals in Life" and should be returned within three weeks."

I was in my last year of high school, and this was one of the first projects we were set to do. It was an easy start for me, because I knew exactly what I wanted to do in life. In fact, it was a continuation of a useful exercise I'd already been doing for myself over the years. I'd started doing drawings of stables and training facilities when I was nine years old.

Given my subject matter, I didn't have to worry about Mr. Fowler's final instruction either, as mine was no Hollywood dream, even though I'd been in countless films by this time. So I pressed ahead with the assignment and turned in what I thought was a good paper on the subject. It was a ground-plan and associated paperwork for the running of a thoroughbred racehorse facility.

Five days later the paper was returned to me with a big red 'F' printed across the top of the page. Also written were the traditional words: "See me." This was a shock, because I was accustomed to achieving good grades. I went immediately to see Mr. Fowler after class, showed him my work again and asked him what in the world I'd done wrong. He leafed through the pages and said, "You know that my last instruction to you was to be realistic in this projection of your future?"

I replied, "Yes, I did realize that."

"Do you realize what the annual income of a person in The United States is?" he asked me.

I replied, "No, I'm sorry but I don't."

"Sixty-three hundred dollars!"

I waited for him to continue, but I had a clear idea of what he was going to say next.

"So how many years would you have to work and save up to earn the amount of money you'd need for your plan?" he asked me.

"I don't know."

He tapped his finger against the red 'F' and advised me, "It is a wild, unattainable dream. That is why I gave it a failing grade based on the instructions that I issued at the outset." Then he handed me back the paper. "I know your family and background; it would just not be possible. Take it home, think about it, change it to an appropriate level and hand it in again. The last thing I want is to fail you based on a misunderstanding."

It felt like he'd driven a knife into me – his reaction was that unexpected. I was suddenly awakened to the reality of finance and I faced the prospect that my dream could never be realized. The next two or three days were depressing. I was at home, agonizing over what to do. I couldn't figure out how I could change it. My mother saw I was troubled and asked what was wrong, so I confided in her.

She read my paper and suggested, "Well, if that's truly your life's dream, then in my opinion you can achieve it. I think you ought to consider turning the paper back in just the way it is, without any changes." She added, "If you think it's unattainable, then you can change it yourself. But I don't think it's for a high school instructor to set a level on your hopes and dreams."

I recall feeling renewed at that point.

I returned to school and handed the paper back the same as before, except with an additional note written on it that his perception as my instructor that it was unattainable was fair enough, but my own was that it was attainable as a life plan, and that I didn't think he had a right to put a cap on my perceptions. He should grade the paper as he thought fit. When the grades were mailed to us, I did get an 'A' for that particular course. I never did find out to what extent he changed the mark, but I couldn't have achieved an 'A' overall if he'd left that paper with an 'F' grade. I didn't know it then, but I was to come into contact with Mr. Lyman Fowler much later in my life, in 1987. Then, the boot would be firmly on the other foot.

QUESTIONS TO PONDER

- Monty communicated honestly and authentically. This approach left a lasting impact on Mr. Fowler. So much so, many years later he returned to Monty's life to admit he had been wrong. In your own life, with whom have you had authentic conversations that have built lasting trust and respect?

- Author Susan Scott suggests that, "Honesty means full disclosure to myself and others, with good intent." Are there relationships in your life that could benefit from such an approach?

How an Authentic Approach Creates Mutual Trust

In the round pen during Join-Up, Monty paces his "conversation" with a horse to ensure that mutual trust develops. Using trust-based communication, he creates a kind of "contract" with the horse so that control is shared and balanced between both parties. The horse "reads" the human's intent. Think about how this relates to your own interactions as a leader or collaborator. If a human leader enters the round pen loaded up with anxiety or anger, the horse will assume that the human is a predictor. Entering a conversation with a neutral stance gives the conversation a chance to start out on a collaborative note. You can think of this conversation as a "trust-based conversation" so that mutual trust is developed.

Monty has commented that, "In order to gain a horse's trust and willing cooperation, it is necessary for both parties to be allowed to meet in the middle. However, it is the responsibility of the man, totally of the man (I'm speaking generically, to include women), to achieve this, and to get to the other side of this hurdle. He can only ever do it by earning the trust of the horse and never abusing its status as a flight animal."

The Join-Up Conversation: A Conversation to Increase Trust

Join-Up is achieved when the horse willingly trusts the human leader. We took a look at the pacing of this round pen "conversation," and broke this process down for human use. Try this approach when you want to build trust and solve problems with another person.

LEARNING TOOL
The Round Pen Trust-Based Conversation Model

In the round pen, Monty develops a two-way conversation with a horse. Perhaps the most important thing he establishes immediately is positive intent. As the "conversation" continues, you can see the stages of Join-Up clearly. The same is true for you engaging in a trust-based conversation. We detail this process in the steps below.

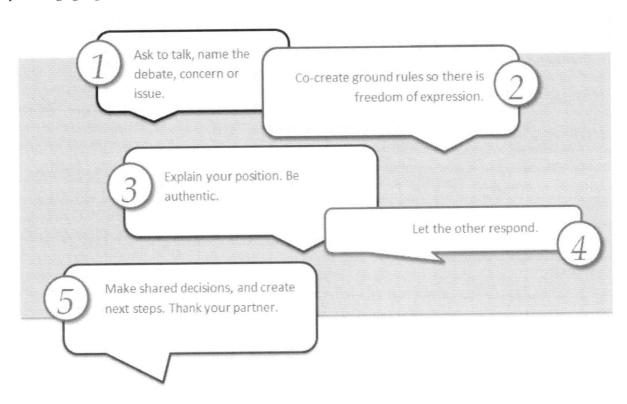

Try holding this conversation with someone whom you have an open issue, or an unresolved concern. Hold the conversation in person, in a private location. To prepare your partner and increase their readiness to trust, request the meeting; don't demand it. Name the issue or concern and share the five steps above with your partner so they understand how the conversation will develop.

Using an Authentic Approach Involves taking a Risk

It's risky to be your authentic self, and with risk come rewards… and more setbacks.

CASE STUDY: *Rebounding by Taking Risks*

Taking risks is an essential skill in rebounding from setbacks. There is a great story about a risk Monty took early in his career. Monty and Pat Roberts paid little attention to the 1960's cultural revolution that swirled around them. As they left college to establish careers in the horse training business, they were busy raising two young children with a third on the way while trying to make ends meet. Monty says:

I believed that, with my reputation, there'd be a lot of horses arriving at any minute. As far as I was concerned, they were already in vans on their way over.

However, they didn't arrive.

We did not have two cents to rub together.

I didn't know what to do about all these horses the owners weren't sending me. I had a few mares to breed and I was giving a few lessons, but it didn't answer the question what to do next. I had only four paid horses in training with me, and I was desperate. I was trying hard for prize money in rodeos, but the figures just didn't add up. I had to find more work.

Someone then gave me a piece of advice: "Go live with Don Dodge for a while."

I knew Don Dodge of course -- everyone did. He was possibly the most successful trainer of horses around, and he really did have a line of vans waiting to turn into his place. The advice given to me was, "Study your ass off with Don. Give him one hundred per cent. If he believes in you, you'll have it made. He'll recommend people to you." Then came the warning…

"Remember he's impossible to impress!" What did I have to lose? I called him up and asked to work for him for a while.

"Yup. Come up if you want. Prepare to go to work, though. You can bring a couple of your own horses, and when it's time for you to leave I'll figure out what you owe me. Cos I'm going to teach you something. God knows you need it!"

The only thing I could afford to eat was a product called MetraCal, which was an all-in-one glue type of substance for people who wanted to lose weight. It cost 90 cents a can, and I lived off it for 10 weeks. Just to look on the bright side for a moment, there were different flavors – I had a choice of Chocolate MetraCal, Vanilla MetraCal or Strawberry MetraCal. You made your decision, and then you had to punch a couple of holes in the top and suck it out of the can.

I had to show up at Don Dodge's at 4:30 in the morning and feed the horses and attend to their stalls. Don would appear at 7:30 and start barking orders. I'd ride a minimum of 10 horses for him during the morning. Then I'd crack another can of MetraCal and keep going. At some point in the afternoon, he'd always spend time with me as I worked on my two horses. He'd shout at the top of his lungs -- he was a hard taskmaster. I bit the bullet; I didn't breathe a word about what I thought, and I just did what I was told.

I learned a lot.

Whenever he was around my two horses, Don Dodge would ask a lot of questions about the other two which I'd left at home. Surrounded by the number he had, it sounded pitiful to talk about the four I had in training. I told him about one of them, a stallion owned by Lawson Williams called Panama Buck, who tried to mate with his reflection if he caught sight of himself in glass. I told him many other details, including who their owners were and how much I was charging for their keep and training. I remember thinking, "Why's he so interested? Does he like hearing about how badly I'm doing?" Then, for the rest of the afternoon Billy and I would be finishing the chores and topping off the stalls and cleaning the tack. We'd be through by 9 p.m.

I'd swallow some more MetraCal and carry on back to Mother Harris' place. Occasionally, Don asked me in for a meal and I fell on the food like the starving person I was. Once or twice we went to a rodeo and I won enough for a few meals, but basically I was on a MetraCal diet. This went on for 10 weeks and I turned into a skeleton; my ribs popped out and I had a deathly pallor. My hands were calloused from the hard work carrying all those buckets, and I was worn down by the constant shouting.

As the time for my departure drew near, Don invited me into his office for a formal meeting to re-cap my visit -- and he warned me he'd be telling me how much I owed him. After his stern treatment of me and my unflagging slave labor for him, I looked forward to the pay-off. Here we go, I thought, he's going to recommend me to everyone he knows and I'll have earned it. He sat down on the opposite side of the desk, stared at me and said, "Well, Monty, I have you figured. You have a little talent, which maybe you could build on. But it's a lot different now. No college bullshit rodeo team."

"No, I realize that, but I hope I'm ready to do it on my own."

"You're going to have to work a lot harder than I've put you through if you want to make any progress at all." I could not believe he'd said that. Suddenly, I was so tired and dispirited I could have beaten him with my fists.

"Now then," he went on, "there is this matter of your promise to do exactly what I instructed."

I nodded in agreement. "Sure." A promise was a promise

He leaned forward and spoke slowly and precisely. "What I want you to do is to go home and call Lawson Williams, and tell him his horse is no good and you're wasting his money. Tell him he's to come and pick him up immediately. Then do the same with that other horse you got back there." I went into a tailspin, hearing this. "How can I do that? I've only got four horses, and you're asking me to cut my income in half? Why? Why on earth should I do such a thing?"

"I don't owe you an explanation, but seeing as you ask – you're going to do it for a very good reason, you're going to do it because he'll be impressed with you. That horse of his isn't going anywhere. You know it; I know it. You'll tell him the truth and he'll respect you for it and send you five horses right back again." I let this sink in. I could see his psychology, but it seemed too risky for someone with only four paid-in-training horses to send two of them away.

"Now," he added, "the reckoning."

I waited for him to congratulate me on my hard work, and he might even judge the poor straits I was in compared with him and press a few dollars into my hand. Instead he said, "You owe me $50 dollars per day; that's a total of $3,200." And he wrote out a bill. "Pay me just as soon as you can. You'll someday realize it's the best bargain you ever had." I drove home with my tail between my legs. When I showed the bill to Pat and told her the story, she was as disappointed as I was.

However, maybe it was because I'd paid so much for this advice that it began to sound good. I started to like the feel of it. It would be a brave thing to do, but I didn't have a lot else to turn to. I delayed for a while, trying to work out the best way of saying it, but there was no other way but head on. I rang Lawson Williams.

"Mr. Williams?"

"Yes?"

"It's Monty Roberts here."

"Hello, Monty. How're things going?"

I hesitated, and then plunged on. "Mr. Williams, I don't want to waste your money, and it's my judgment that Panama Buck isn't worth spending any more on. I'd like you to come down and collect –"Lawson Williams interrupted me, "You useless son of a gun, you wouldn't know a good horse if it leapt up between your legs. That's the last horse you'll ever get from me!" Then he slammed down his receiver, and the next day a man arrived to take Panama Buck.

Great! Now I really couldn't feed my wife and children. We'd all be on MetraCal now.

Shortly afterwards Selah Reed, the one paid horse-in-training I had with any promise, broke her hind leg and had to be put down. I was running on empty. I was so low that I literally walked about the place thinking about suicide the whole time. It was going badly wrong and I was letting my family down. It wasn't worth carrying on.

Then I received a telephone call.

"Hello. Mr. Gray here, Joe Gray. I'm a contractor laying pipelines."

"Hello, Mr. Gray." Who was this guy?

"I was having lunch with Mr. Williams yesterday. He was complaining about you, but from what I heard you must be about the only honest horse trainer I ever heard of."

A wave of emotion overtook me. I remembered Don Dodge's intense stare, and his advice and the MetraCal. Everything came flooding back, and I sensed it was all going to pay off.

"What can I do for you, Mr. Gray?"

"Well, I know that Panama Buck horse of his wasn't any good, and I just want to take a flyer on you. I have this horse I want to send you; it's called My Blue Heaven." The feeling in my heart was that I'd turned a corner and I could glimpse daylight.

QUESTIONS TO PONDER

- In light of his later success, how would you evaluate the risk Monty took?

- What risks have you taken that led to later success?

- Are there any risks you've been avoiding? If taken, could they lead to breakthroughs like Monty's?

LESSON THREE TAKE-AWAYS

- Setbacks create learning opportunities that are cleverly disguised opportunities for personal growth.

- Standing up for yourself and stating your true feelings through confident communication is more useful than avoiding, backing down, or attacking others.

- Taking risks is uncomfortable, but it is the only way to grow, learn, and achieve your goals.

Notes:

"The feeling in my heart was that I'd turned a corner and I could glimpse daylight."

- Monty Roberts

LESSON 4

Why Values Matter

"I would find my fiber tested as never before, I would find what friends are made of, and I would find the courage to continue."

-Monty Roberts

In Chapter Four, *The Sandcastle Syndrome*, Monty's career spins into high gear with a partnership that sends him to new heights, and plunges him into murky depths. Monty built his dream thoroughbred breeding and training farm with a partner who was determined to ruin his success. See if you can place the importance of Monty's convictions as he is forced to make life-changing decisions.

The entrance to Flag Is Up Farms

The Importance of Values

"Your beliefs become your thoughts,
Your thoughts become your words,
Your words become your actions,
Your actions become your habits,
Your habits become your values,
Your values become your destiny."

- Mahatma Gandhi

We each make many decisions every day, and most of us don't think about what we base them on. Beneath these decisions (even seemingly casual ones) lay our reasons, or values. Your values are good to know, because they help you direct your energy toward what you feel is important. Sometimes it's incredibly inconvenient to have values at all -- and more often than not, they show up in situations you are least prepared to handle.

This story has to do with Monty following his business partner into a ruinous situation, and having the courage to make critical decisions based on personal values rather than reacting to pressure:

In 1964, when I was 31 years old, I encountered a man who would change our lives forever. He would take my family and me to the heights of success . . . and then bring us way lower than we'd ever have imagined possible.

The man's name was Hastings Harcourt, son of the founder of the publishers Harcourt Brace & World. The prospect that Harcourt was offering me was in a different league, but I felt that Pat and I had the necessary talent and he was a man who could give us the chance we needed to prove ourselves. It had been my life's dream to be a part of a horse operation in the Santa Ynez Valley.

Mr. Harcourt was full of plans. "Start studying the area," he advised, "and I will purchase enough property to encompass a world-class facility." I responded immediately and went at it with the youthful enthusiasm you might have expected from a 31-year-old who had dreamed of doing just this for as far back as he could remember.

As his business relationship with Harcourt developed, Monty found himself often wondering about Harcourt's emotional stability. Despite this concern, the project lurched forward. Not only was Monty's life ambition taking shape in front of his very eyes, it was also a perfect home for his family. They were up and running!

We moved the first horses onto the farm in July 1966.

In October of the same year, our family moved into a beautiful new home overlooking the farm and the Santa Ynez Valley. As far as we were concerned, we'd stepped into paradise. One day, Mr. Harcourt came to the house and started to confide in me about his psychological problems. As a result of this condition, he'd suffered from manic depression from a very early age.

I felt sorry for him, but I didn't know how I could help.

In his business relationships, though, he said that people bumped up against these mood swings of his and were defeated by the experience. "They're being logical; you know when I'm not being logical," he said.

Monty soon found himself in a losing proposition. Harcourt wanted to divest himself of the expansive property and business he had so zealously built with Monty. While Monty was willing to comply, Harcourt's plans went beyond that. He wanted the horses at Flag Is Up Farms destroyed.

This had turned into the firestorm, the melt-down I'd been waiting for. I no longer felt amazement, or sorrow, or incomprehension. I felt anger and determination. I wouldn't let this happen. No horse that I looked after was going to be sacrificed on the whim of an unstable man. I felt renewed incomprehension of Mr. Harcourt's actions. What was going on inside that man's head? And how would he react if he found out I'd refused to destroy his horses? As a matter of ethics, I took the position that he was a sick man making irrational decisions, and I simply could not allow the animals to be the victims of this malady.

Early the following morning, I received a telephone call.

"Mr. Roberts?" It was a woman's voice, normal and unconcerned, the sort of voice you'd hear on the other end of some complaint you were making about a dishwasher you'd bought which didn't work.

"Speaking."

"I'm calling on behalf of Hastings Harcourt."

"Yes."

"Can you confirm for me that the horse named Travel's Echo has been destroyed?"

I needed to lie, but I found it sticking in my throat. I'd never been in a situation where it was demanded of me to deceive anyone. Yet now it was utterly important.

"Yes, he's gone."

"And the two colts, Veiled Wonder and Cherokee Arrow, have they also been destroyed?"

"Yes, I can confirm they've gone too."

"And can you confirm that Mrs. Harcourt's driving ponies have also been destroyed?"

"Yes. They're no longer here."

"And lastly, I need to confirm that you personally undertook the disposal of these animals."

"Yes."

"Thank you, Mr. Roberts." The phone clicked and the disembodied voice was gone.

QUESTIONS TO PONDER

- Monty had to make decisions quickly, under enormous pressure. While he was willing to comply with Harcourt's early request to liquidate their mutual business, he reached a bottom-line decision when it came to destroying the horses. In your own life, what are your "bottom lines?"

- Monty followed his values and made choices based on them. When is the last time you acted on your values? What happened as a result?

LEARNING TOOL
Steps to Defining Your Core Values
Defining Your Values

Defining your values allows you to discover what is truly important. A great way to begin this process is by reviewing your life's roadmap, identifying the choices that worked well and provided affirmation that you had made a good choice.

STEP 1 — Identify times in your life when you were at your happiest-what were you doing, who were you with, why was it such a happy time?

STEP 2 — Identify things you are most proud of that you have done or experienced. Who were you with? Did anyone else affirm your sense of pride?

STEP 3 — Identify times when you felt most fulfilled or satisfied-what needs did these times meet? Why were these times meaningful?

STEP 4 — Determine your top values, based on your experiences of happiness, pride, and fulfillment.

STEP 5 — Prioritize Your Values

- Write each value or value phrase down on a notecard.
- Then arrange the cards in front of you in a line, in no particular order.
- Force yourself to reassign them in order of importance, from most to least importance.
- Place values of equal importance side by side.
- Work through your list and compare each value to others until your list is in the correct order.

STEP 6 — Check your list-do your values seem to be in the right order for you? Do you feel that this order represents your true values, and would you be willing to proclaim them to others?

Take a look at the list you compiled. What values keep popping out at you? Now make a list of all the values you see.

LESSON FOUR TAKE-AWAYS

- Values are the basis for many of your decisions, and make your approach unique.

- Knowing your values allows you to align your actions around what is important.

Notes:

"It isn't the great trainer who can cause a horse to perform. It is the great trainer who can cause a horse to want to perform."

-Monty Roberts

LESSON 5

Acceptance -
A Useful Coping Tool

"I was keen to get back to what I was good at - horses."

-Monty Roberts

In Chapter Five, *Flag Is Up Farms Regained*, we get a glimpse of a man who has survived an epic ordeal - losing his home and business and regaining it once again. We learn about the numbing feeling of relief, of accepting what comes, and of maintaining hope despite the odds.

Monty and Shy Boy with some of his young students.

Letting Go of Control That Isn't Working: The Power of Acceptance

"Because one believes in oneself, one doesn't try to convince others. Because one is content with oneself, one doesn't need others' approval. Because one accepts oneself, the whole world accepts him or her."

- Lao Tzu

It takes a lot of determination to get through the setbacks in our lives. How can we sustain momentum when we are experiencing setbacks? From psychology, we learn that acceptance (the willingness to let go of control) helps us manage the inevitable down times. Monty was exhausted by his terrifying ordeal with Harcourt Hastings, and the resulting life-changing trial. When a judge was hauled out of retirement to settle the case, Monty emerged victorious.

Despite the fact that he'd won back Flag Is Up Farms, Monty faced daunting opposition from his father. The affirmation he had once longed for had since mellowed into a wary acceptance of his father's cool rejection.

CASE STUDY: *Accepting What You Can't Change*

"Resentment is like taking poison and waiting for the other person to die."

- **Malachy McCourt**

My parents came to stay. This was increasingly unusual, and the fact that they were to be here for as long as a week told us that my mother's cancer was probably worse.

We judged that she was making a last-ditch effort before she died to patch up the relationship between her husband and her son.

There was no doubt about it, she engineered for my father to watch me work in the round pen. She made sure of my schedule before they came, she organized a stool for him to sit on, she made sure he couldn't wriggle out of it. She near as anything told him he had to sit there and take note of what I was doing and acknowledge that it was working.

So my father sat there on his stool, ready to watch me start a raw horse. He was well into his seventies and, as I've mentioned before, his opinion was irrelevant to me on the surface of things. After all, I'd started over 6,500 horses by this time, and above and beyond the working horses I'd trained some wonderful thoroughbreds who'd gone on to win at some of the top racing fixtures in the world. I wasn't a youngster desperate for his approval; I was a man in my forties who wanted his parents to feel comfortable with each other and with their son.

Nevertheless, I also wanted to give it my best shot and finally show him what I'd achieved through many long years of working with horses and – more recently – the deer.

Monty proceeded to start a young filly while his father looked on.

I checked my watch. "Half an hour," I called to my father as he sat on his stool. "Which is about average."

By the end of the day, my father had seen me start more horses than he would have believed possible to 'break' in six weeks. He came down from the viewing deck and we stood outside, hardly able to see each other's faces in the gloom.

My mother called to him, "What d'you think of that?"

But he couldn't let go of his way of life. Even faced with such proof as I'd shown him again and again, it was too much to ask of him to admit the old ways weren't the best ways. He replied,

"It's suicide! They'll kill him if he keeps doing it that way."

QUESTIONS TO PONDER

- Acceptance of things we cannot change helps to release us and redirect energy into other situations. Take an inventory of situations you are trying to change. Which of these offer fresh opportunities to accept "unchangeables" and move on? Which can you recommit to?

- How did Monty cope with his father? Do you have people in your life that have difficulty affirming you? What can you do to cope more effectively?

LESSON FIVE TAKE-AWAYS

- Acceptance is a process.

- Trying to change the "unchangeables" in life will drain your energy.

- Accepting "unchangeables" will free up energy to be used elsewhere.

Notes:

"I was, therefore, from a very early age looking for a way to build a trusting relationship, a 50–50 partnership. Through my observation of the Mustangs in the desert and being constantly around horses, it occurred to me, as I watched them moving about in a close-knit herd united for survival, that trust and communication were the keys to their success as a species. After much observation, I could put the rudiments of their language together. I believed that if the horse could trust me, then the whole learning process would speed up. I felt strongly that the answer was through communication. It was many years before I could share my methods with the public. I produced good horses and no one knew how. After my father died, I went public. The rest is history."

-Monty Roberts

LESSON 6

Vulnerability -
The Gateway to Compassion

"I think of myself as multi-lingual...I speak English, a better than passable horse, and I get along quite nicely in deer."

-Monty Roberts

In Chapter Six, *Deer Friends*, we see Monty's deep appreciation for the deer as a flight animal. Part tonic, part seductive-puzzle, deer to Monty represent the quest for the ultimate **Join-Up**. See if you can find how acknowledging vulnerability plays a role in developing compassion.

Monty practicing interspecies communication

Vulnerability -
Birthplace of Innovation, Creativity and Change

"What happens when people open their hearts?"
"They get better."

- Haruki Murakam

Monty has long been drawn to deer, the ultimate flight animal. At his home on any given day, deer are gathered outside his front door. He likens their flight mechanism to horses, except they are a hundred fold more sensitive. He has nurtured relationships with a multitude of deer, and believes "we have too long underestimated the intelligence and acuity of deer."

From Chapter Six, we learn that injured deer often show up on Monty's lawn. Respect for vulnerability is hard to cultivate in our culture. Vulnerability is often seen as something to hide; a weakness. But vulnerability is the gateway to compassion and what author Brene Brown calls "the birthplace of innovation, creativity, and change."

She writes:

"Nothing has transformed my life more than realizing that it's a waste of time to evaluate my worthiness by weighing the reaction of the people in the stands. The people who love me and will be there regardless of the outcome are within arm's reach. This realization changed everything."

CASE STUDY: *An Environment that Supports Vulnerability*

Monty is respected the world over by those who see great value in his ideas. It is a stunning realization to think that a twelve hundred pound horse is a flight animal. He sums up his perspective on respecting horses' vulnerability and their training needs this way:

The creation of willingness within your horse is possible only in an environment free of fear and resentment. To create a place free of these two elements, you must eliminate violence and force as an option and establish parameters of cooperation using discipline that is acceptable and bilaterally agreeable.

QUESTIONS TO PONDER

- In what ways are your vulnerabilities the best part of you?

- What would it take to accept them or even appreciate them?

LESSON SIX TAKE-AWAYS

- Vulnerability is shared by all living things.

- We often protect our vulnerability in ways that are not useful to us.

- Violence is never an effective means to meet the needs of a vulnerable person or animal.

Notes:

"For centuries, humans have said to horses, you do what I tell you or I'll hurt you. Humans still say that to each other, still threaten, force, and intimidate. I'm convinced that my discovery with horses also has value in the workplace, in the educational and penal systems and in raising children. At heart, I'm saying no one has the right to say, "You must" to an animal, or to another human."

-Monty Roberts

LESSON 7

Affirmation -
The Fuel that Builds Self-Worth

"This second life of mine has taken me to more than 30 countries, and this book has been translated into 14 languages. While I would like to see still further changes and a still better existence for these wonderful partners of ours, I could never have dreamed that so much could have been accomplished in such a short period of time."

-Monty Roberts

In Chapter Seven, *The Invitation That Changed My Life*, we find Monty meeting the Queen of England and converting disbelievers to the use of non-violence in training horses. What values underlie Monty's steadfast commitment to his training methods, and why does he persist despite the challenges he faces?

Monty and Her Majesty Queen Elizabeth II

The Value of Affirmation

"If you think you can do a thing or think you can't do a thing, you're right."

- Henry Ford

In his book, *How Full is Your Bucket?* Author Tom Rath talks about the value of affirmation and the impact it can have on relationships, productivity, health, and longevity. He makes the case that many of us have a metaphorical bucket. Others can "dip" from or "replace" our buckets, leaving us emotionally depleted or charged-up. We do the same for others. The point is that validation, recognition, and affirmation build and stabilize self-worth. How often have you forgotten to do for others what Monty suggests: "Catch your horse doing something right?" A simple comment, a voiced approval, a note of thanks. These small but emotionally significant gestures serve as emotional reference points. From Chapter Seven, we learn that after years of struggle, Monty finally received his own bucket-filler.

CASE STUDY: *On the Need for Validation and Recognition*

In April 1989, I was invited to go to England to give a demonstration of my work in front of Her Majesty Queen Elizabeth II, Prince Philip, and the Queen Mother. The impact of this visit on me can be imagined. It was as though I was finally allowed out into the daylight, blinking a bit in the fierce glare of publicity -- but with my work recognized as valid and genuine. It wasn't long, it must be remembered, since I'd built the viewing deck above the round pen at Flag Is Up; before that, I didn't show what I could do to anyone, because I thought it had been proved to me that people wouldn't accept it. Now, one of the most important figures in the horse world —and I mean world — was actively taking part in promoting demonstrations of my work to members of the public.

QUESTIONS TO PONDER

- What affect did the Queen's invitation have on Monty's sense of personal validity?

- Has anyone affirmed you in a way that made you feel personal validation?

- Are there people who could benefit from your validation?

CASE STUDY: *When Others Dip from Your Self-Worth Bucket*

Monty received a phone call that would change his life. Queen Elizabeth II of England had heard about Monty's methods. She invited him to England to give a demonstration. Once he arrived and had successfully demonstrated a Join-Up, some disbelief still remained.

I would learn that the Queen had spoken with her staff and they'd suggested to her that I had done something underhanded with the horses when I was supposedly taking them through the ring to acclimatize them. In short, they suspected some form of trickery.

The Queen hadn't agreed with their judgment but, nonetheless, she'd asked what they would need to see in order to be convinced that my work wasn't fraudulent.

They'd suggested that a truck be sent over to Hampton Court to pick up two very large, three-year-old Piebald stallions, who were very raw and had barely been handled; they'd certainly never seen me or the round pen. They proposed to take them one at a time off the truck and see if I could start them – predicting I would fail.

Sir John told me he wanted me to start these horses without acclimatizing them to the ring. Because my working methods were new to him, I suppose it didn't seem like much of a request. However, it's unfair to expect horses to go through an experience that must rank as the most traumatic of their lives and be introduced to a frightening new environment at the same time.

This new plan concerned me, as there was enough pressure on the event already. I was in a fishbowl. It was important that everything went well, and naturally I wanted the right measures taken to give me the best chance. There were 100 guests invited to see the demonstration that afternoon, as well as the stable staff who were now lining up against the wall, and I knew they were expecting me to fail so my work would be judged as false.

Sir John took the microphone and stepped into the round pen to introduce me. The huge Piebald colt came charging towards him and slapped his big front feet on the ground, exhibiting anger over the whole situation. So, Sir John stepped quickly back outside the gate and made the introduction from the other side of the fence – and you couldn't blame him.

I was not happy about these new circumstances, which I felt were unfair as well as dangerous. This big colt was aggressive and, in addition, continually distracted by his friend's calling from just outside the building. Suddenly, everyone stood up – the Queen had walked in. She wasn't scheduled to be here, but she had turned up to see the outcome of this. She went to an area behind where the seats were located and gestured to everyone that they might sit down.

Sir John continued with his introductory speech and explained what they were about to see. I couldn't do much else but step through the gate into the round pen, pick up my line and give it a go.

QUESTIONS TO PONDER

- When others don't believe in you, what have you done?

- What does taking a risk or "giving it a go" under pressure take?

- Life is messy. Sometimes success brings more messes. What are your thoughts on the messiness and demands success has brought to your life?

CASE STUDY: *Acknowledging Success*

As the Oxfordshire hedgerows slid past the windows of our vehicle, I could hardly believe it – we were going to show what I could do to people all over Britain. In 1966, when I'd built the round pen at Flag Is Up Farms, I'd designed it without a viewing balcony so no one could see in. Since the time I'd shown Ray Hackworth what I could do with starting the Mustangs in the mid-1940s, I'd shown my work to no one; not until the mid-1980s. Now I was going to drive hundreds of miles every day in a foreign country to show as many people as possible. I was actively seeking their support and approval.

The response I received was incredible.

In Newmarket, we found five of the wildest two- and three-year-olds you could ever imagine. They were just a tick quieter than Mustangs would be, extremely raw and green, but they were very healthy and well-fed. The weather was hostile -- driving wind and rain on the second day -- and I couldn't imagine that people would stand there and watch me start these "wild horses," but they did; there must have been 200-300 people there. They braved that weather unbelievably and the horses went well. One of them was filmed by Channel 4, which televised it all over the British Isles. Sheik Mohammed and a contingent of people from the Arab Emirates came, and I'm told they liked what they saw. We stayed at Sandringham, on the Queen's property, with Michael Osborne and his wife. They had a wonderful dinner party arranged, and I had many questions to answer.

As I was enjoying this day and thinking about everything that had happened, I realized that it had been one of the most rewarding times of my life. The pressure had gone, and our visit had been a success. It had been a storybook week for myself, my family, and Sean.

Peter Block is a gifted best-selling author. He defines himself as a "citizen of Cincinnati, Ohio." He often writes about consumerism and how it lulls people into the role of passive observer. In his mind, it is critically important to transform people's thinking from being a consumer to becoming proactive, participating citizens. The themes in his writings help individuals validate themselves and take ownership and responsibility for their lives. Block says that, "All we have to do to create the future is to change the nature of our conversations, to go from blame to ownership, and from bargaining to commitment, and from problem solving to possibilities thinking." Perhaps the most important conversation starts with you. What active role could you take in committing to the possibilities in your future?

QUESTIONS TO PONDER

- What about you? Think about the most rewarding times in your life. How did you acknowledge them? Did you celebrate?

- What value would increasing celebrations have in your life

CASE STUDY: *Celebrating Success - A Way to Self-Validate*

We live in a culture that constantly scrutinizes our success or failure. The little meter in your head that keeps track of accomplishments can be quite unforgiving and has a long memory. As we have learned, self -affirmation is an important component of building self-worth. Changing the conversation that you are having with yourself and validating your strengths and abilities is a very important skill to develop. From strengths-based research, we know that focusing on our weaknesses and attempting to improve them is far less effective than building on our strengths. Clifton and Hodges define a strength as the ability to provide consistent, near-perfect performance in a given activity. They found that the key is to first identify your dominant talent themes which occur naturally within you, then refine these with the skills and knowledge that is only reachable outside of you.

QUESTIONS TO PONDER

- What natural strengths do you have?

- How can these strengths allow you to actively pursue the possibilities that exist in your future?

_____

_____

_____

_____

_____

_____

_____

_____

_____

_____

_____

LEARNING TOOL
Personal Gifts Inventory

> What do you count among your key accomplishments?

> What permission are you withholding from yourself that could help you acknowledge your own successes?

> You have gifts that others may have discouraged, or that go unappreciated or unnoticed. What are they?

> How can you begin to bring these gifts forward, and perhaps try again or push past boundaries?

Monty had internal talents that were refined by his life experiences. When Monty roamed the high desert plains watching Mustang, or was riding the rodeo circuit, he was escaping his father's brutality. He was taking a natural talent and refining it with skills and knowledge. His gifts and talents were so discouraged that he hid his round pen discoveries away for many years. His discoveries really mattered to him, and with persistence and determination, he refined his talent until he became an expert at starting horses.

Take a minute to think about this quote: "Nothing you do matters until everything you do counts." Author Umami Haque believes that "...every kind of institution - business or otherwise - today carries not just a social responsibility, but an existential responsibility." This is a responsibility not just to society, but to life itself; and further, to the art of living. An obligation to elevate what's worthy, good and true in every life; a duty not to just "serve" people as "consumers", but to better people as humans; a calling not merely to "deliver", but to matter. Monty believed that his work had meaning, even when others did not.

CASE STUDY: *Monty schools his audience on why non-violence in training matters*

It was in Scotland that Sean said something which made me laugh. He'd just ridden a four-year-old stallion – an aggressive animal, as I remember 16.2 hands high and over 1,200 pounds in weight, full of grain. When he caved in and forgot about being a stallion, this horse went like a charm. Up on his back for the first time, Sean could relax, and he called to me in a loud voice,

"Fifty-first fluke in a row!"

I had to explain my laughter to the audience. "You know," I said, "every place we go, there's always someone who says that what they're watching must be a fluke. It's become a standing joke, that there's always a person who says it was a fluke. New audience, new fluke! Well, as Sean mentioned just then, this is our fifty-first fluke in a row in this country –and I'm not even counting the many thousands of horses I've started before I landed at Heathrow!"

QUESTIONS TO PONDER

- What are the "flukes" in your life that are were actually caused by your strengths?

- When others refuse to acknowledge your strengths, what can you do to cope?

- How can identifying and valuing your strengths help you cope when others don't believe in you?

Believe in Your Strengths and Others Will, Too

After his initial success with the Queen's demonstration, Monty was invited to give demonstrations in Ireland. He was presented with a young, aggressive colt who had not been started.

I asked Hugh McCusker about the history of this colt, Stanley, but he wasn't sure what had been done with him before; only that he'd never been saddled, bridled, or ridden. When everyone heard that Stanley was going to be started without a lead rope attached to his head, they'd all gone and telephoned their friends to tell them to come and see this cowboy get eaten alive!

Having probably 600 people watching him, Stanley marched around the pen and appeared very much in charge of the situation. I didn't need to be told that this was a colt with some reputation.

I switched on my lapel microphone and announced to the crowd that I was ready to go ahead. As I walked towards the gate leading into the round pen, you could have heard a pin drop. Suddenly there wasn't a single person rustling a crisp packet, nor a single cough.

I opened the gate and stepped into the pen. At that time Stanley was on the far side, about 50 feet from me. As I closed the gate behind me and stepped away from the fence, he arched his neck and marched about three steps towards me. Then he pinned his ears back, bared his teeth and came at me, full-speed. The audience gasped. I tripped the latch on the gate and stepped outside. The colt slammed to a halt inches from the fence and turned away to show off his supremacy.

I said to the audience, "Wow! What are you trying to do to me here?" I shook my head and put my hands on my hips, looking around at the banks of people sitting and staring. "Surely the nice people of Ireland wouldn't set me up for something like this, would they, by any chance?"

Not a word was spoken, and not a sound could be heard.

I stood there for a while, then I sat down on a chair near my gate and gave the impression that I was very worried about going into the pen and dealing with this horse. Then I addressed the audience again. I said, "On this trip I've met a lot of skeptical Irish horsemen who feel that some of my work is less than believable. Now, I know that Ireland is filled with good horsemen – in fact, I'm sure there are a lot of them in the building right now. And since I'm a 56-year-old man who's completely out of shape and has had half his backbone surgically removed, I'd very much like to ask for a volunteer to come and deal with this horse. It would be interesting to see what an Irish horseman could do with a horse as aggressive as this."

I sat there for a few seconds and listened to this deep silence. To tell the truth, I wanted to see a few red faces. And then I said in a surprised voice, "No volunteers? Come on, think about it. Let's get some young kid down here who's in good shape, and he can go ahead and do this horse. I'll make some suggestions from outside the ring."

Again there was not a motion, nor a sound. It was absolutely dead silent in that room, except for the sound of the colt's breath and his giant foot pawing at the floor of the round pen.

Then I said, "Well, I guess I'm going to have to go ahead and start him myself." I went to my equipment bag and got out my nylon lariat rope, leaving my light sash line outside the pen.

QUESTIONS TO PONDER

- When presented with disbelief and opposition, what did Monty do?

- How did turning the tables to invite participation impact people's resistance?

- What impact did believing in his strengths and beliefs have on Monty's situation?

LESSON SEVEN TAKE-AWAYS

- In *How Full Is Your Bucket*, Tom Rath explains that we all have an "emotional bucket" that others can "dip" or "replace" from.

- When others "dip" or "replace" from our bucket, we feel emotionally depleted or charged.

- Affirmation, validation, and recognition build and stabilize self-worth.

- Self -affirmation is an important component of self-worth

Notes:

"A horse trainer must keep in mind the idea that the horse can do no wrong; and any action taken by the horse, especially the young unstarted horse, was most likely influenced by you."

- Monty Roberts

LESSON 8
Putting it All Together

"Our mission is to become a world leader in developing programs that utilize the trust-based philosophy and training of Join-Up. We will share these innovative methods to foster collaborative environments which cultivate and nurture teambuilding, leadership and performance skills."

- Monty Roberts on the Mission of Join-Up International

In Chapter Eight, *When a Racehorse's Worst Nightmare is a Starting Gate,* we see the collective wisdom of a man who has learned, taught, sorted-through, and applied years of knowledge, only to be stumped by new challenges. The book leaves us abruptly, like a good conversation that you wish wouldn't end. What about you? What have you learned from these chapters?

The first saddle of this horse's life

The Importance of Pivotal Events

Take a look at the roadmap you have created in your life. What pivotal events occurred as you developed? As you achieved your dreams and suffered through your setbacks?

"You must begin to think of yourself as becoming the person you want to be."

- David Viscott

CASE STUDY: *Know Your Pivotal Events*

Monty took stock of his life's roadmap. Take a look at what he came up with:

There are events for all of us which serve to change the pattern of our lives. The first of which, for me, was in 1943 when my father killed the black man. I remember the second of these as being my conversation with Brownie in 1948. The third was on 16 June 1956, when I married Pat. Her support and her tolerance for my shortcomings, failings, and maniacal approach to my work is absolutely essential, I know now. Somehow I was lucky enough to find that person at the first attempt. Then, as I said earlier, the birth of our children – Debbie on 10 April 1957, Lori on 12 January 1959 and Marty on 1 February 1961 – these were events that changed the character of my life. In dealing with horses, there was my life before Johnny Tivio and my life after him. I've never dealt with a horse with the kind of brain that Johnny Tivio had. He was the one who trained me– not vice versa. Then perhaps there is the Monty Roberts before April of 1989, when I spent my first week with the Queen and her family, and there's a different Monty Roberts afterwards.

QUESTIONS TO PONDER

- What are your critical pivotal events?

- Can you list them, and reflect on how they changed your life?

- What's ahead for you? How will that change you?

Sometimes pivotal points in our lives occur because we made a discovery that changes everything. When success comes from failures it means that we had the determination to rebound from failure and learn from it. Having the curiosity, resilience, and determination to learn from failures creates the pivotal learning lessons in our lives.

Innovation Comes from Failure (Read; Learning)

"Believing there is a solution paves the way to a solution."

- Dr. David Schwartz

From Chapter Eight, we learn that Monty has worked with many horses needing remedial work. Helping them face their fears, phobias, and numerous deep-seated concerns has been a large part of his career. In England, Monty worked with a horse named Prince of Darkness. After a first attempt to work with his starting gate claustrophobia, Monty returned home. His client, Sir Mark Prescott called Monty from England to let him know that Prince of Darkness was again failing at the racecourse starting gate.

I stand behind the work I do. Sir Mark agreed to fly me back to England on a no-fee basis, to deal with the problem. So here I was, back again, with a real puzzle that was keeping us all awake in the middle of the night.

I puzzled about the psychology of it – where was the fear coming from? If I could find the source of his fear, I'd be home and dry. It wasn't claustrophobia, there was something about the starting stall which spooked him, but I couldn't find out what it was.

That night I really wanted to tell Sir Mark I was going to have to quit and refund him the money, but I just couldn't get the words out. The thought of losing was killing me. We had been there three days and I didn't feel any closer to success. I decided to give it one more try.

After many iterations of trial and error learning, Monty finally encountered success.

I stood there, bruised, battered, with a trickle of blood running into my collar, but I'd found it: the source of his fear was the rail itself – of course! A trailer has smooth sides to the stall, whereas the starting stalls have rails running along each side. That must be the difference. I could have kicked myself for not realizing sooner, but I felt a sudden excitement that I'd found out what he was afraid of. It was that specific. Something in the character of those foot rails running along the inside caused him great fear. After a few tests, I knew I was right. I was lucky to still have both my ears attached to my head and no broken bones, but I had the answer: if it wasn't for those rails along the side of the stalls, he could be raced tomorrow.

That evening Sir Mark and I discussed the situation, and with mounting excitement he phoned the various racing officials to investigate the possibility of removing the rails from inside a given starting stall.

Monty got busy. He became passionately curious about the horse's phobia. He began to realize the horse's fear came from the rear rails of a racing starting gate. Monty threw himself into the task.

I outlined an idea that was going through my mind. If we could manufacture something like the picador's horse wears in the bullfighting ring – a drape made of heavy leather to go over his rear quarters, heavy enough to protect his flanks – then we could maybe convince him he had enough protection from those evil rails. It was just a wild thought, and I didn't really think it would be practical. I felt that if I could use something like this to protect Prince of Darkness' sides from those rails, he might accept the stalls.

Geraldine Rees said, "What if we used carpet?"

All kinds of flashing lights went off in my head. Using carpet instead of heavy leather might be a practical solution. So we jumped into her car, went into Newmarket and bought a roll of remnant carpet. Then we went to Gibson's Saddlery and I started to design the kind of thing I thought might work.

When I put him in the starting stalls with his special blanket on, I immediately knew we were on the right track.

The more he rubbed against the sides of the stall, stepping backwards and forwards, the more Prince of Darkness realized that he had protection from the rails. He relaxed and calmed down. We were making progress.

I didn't know it then, but this experience would lead me to invent 'The Monty Roberts blanket' for horses with similar fears. It has now been used on more than 1000 horses.

QUESTIONS TO PONDER

- What role did failure play in this story?

- Gordon Moore, co-founder of Intel Corporation says, "If everything you try works, you are not trying hard enough." How about you? Do you step out of your comfort zone often enough?

- In your life have you felt like quitting?

- When you persisted (instead of quitting,) what happened?

Coming Full Circle

One of the most remarkable things about Monty's life is that he started a second career after age 50. He is a great role model for many people working past retirement age who hope for personal development and interesting career opportunities. His emphasis on being a humble and gentle leader offer insights for business professionals looking to be authentic leaders. His compassionate approach to starting horses lets us know more about how to collaborate with others using a trust-based approach. In your own life, what new appreciation do you have for the challenges you have had to overcome? What strengths have you re-embraced? What thinking have you done on your need for more affirmation?

This book has allowed us to have an extended conversation about your own purpose and how to deepen it despite the odds.

Learning Tool
Personal Development Plan

Circle back to the first learning tool that you completed-the **Personal Strengths Shield**. Then review the learning tools that you completed after that. What patterns have emerged? What areas of strength do you have that will be there as you write your own life chapters in the years ahead? Here is a tool, a personal development chart, to get started. What priorities do you see? How will you know that you have achieved your goals in these areas?

Personal Development Plan

Think about your near-term priorities that will result in the most gain. Then use this plan as a blueprint to develop the next chapter of your life!

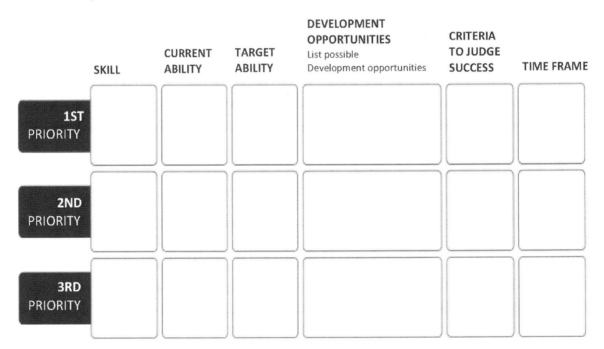

	SKILL	CURRENT ABILITY	TARGET ABILITY	DEVELOPMENT OPPORTUNITIES List possible Development opportunities	CRITERIA TO JUDGE SUCCESS	TIME FRAME
1ST PRIORITY						
2ND PRIORITY						
3RD PRIORITY						

LESSON EIGHT TAKE-AWAYS

- Knowing your pivotal events can inform you about what experiences you had in your life that developed you into the person you are today.

- Monty's ability to learn from failure led him to invent the "Monty Roberts Blanket" for horses.

- Think about how you can apply your key learning's to your life.

Download a paper copy of the Life Lessons Toolkit to use at:
http://corplearning.com/life-lessons_resources.html

Post comments about your own journey ahead on our Facebook page at:
https://www.facebook.com/LifeLessonsFromTheManWhoListensToHorses?ref=hl

Notes:

"Many people watch, but few see."

- **Monty Roberts**

Congratulations!

This completed field guide can serve as reference manual for you -- a guide for looking back and looking ahead. Refer to it often, and remember that each new learning lesson will arrive cleverly disguised as a challenge or problem to solve. Keep us posted on your journey by visiting our Facebook page at:

https://www.facebook.com/LifeLessonsFromTheManWhoListensToHorses?ref=hl

Monty on one of his favorite mounts, Nice Chrome.

"The major source of satisfaction that I received from working with horses is the verification by the horses of what my work means to them."

- Monty Roberts

Afterword...

On an ordinary day recently, I drove into Flag Is Up Farms, past the electronic gate that swings open, down the long entry road lined with trees that gently arch over it, and into the staff parking area. That day I walked the fields and paddocks of Flag Is Up Farms, recalling the stories from Monty's books, and thinking about the land that they all occurred on. I saw ancient horses living out their last days in peaceful paddocks, young horses playing in the greenest fields, and everywhere, a peaceful quiet sensation. I walked past Shy Boy, past Nice Chrome in his stall and the fields and racetrack, and then came to settle on something I had not seen before. It was a gentling pen, a kind of small round pen shrunk down to a miniature size with a fenced shoot extended from it. I asked what the purpose was, and I was told to that it helped acclimate wild horses to human touch. Horses could enter the pen from a trailer or adjoining paddock without force or trauma. I thought about the gentling pen. Then I thought about how many of us could use our own gentling pens, and how useful it could be if we stopped to consider how to create more gentling pens in our lives. I walked back to my car, got in and drove off down the long entryway with its glimpses of pasture. The gate swung open to let me out, but I knew I'd be back, at least in my mind, when I needed to recover from the traumas, real or imagined, in my own life. We hope that this book serves you well as your own gentling pen.

Sue and Debbie

Interactive Map of Flag Is Up Farms

WELCOME TO

FLAG IS UP FARMS

Monty & Pat Roberts

Please do not feed the horses or enter the training barns, stalls, paddocks, or pastures.

◄ BUELLTON   HWY 246   SOLVANG ►

1 Visitor's Center	**4** Round Pen/School Yard	**7** Western Arena/Cutting Pens	**12** Gravesites
2 Student Center	**5** Shy Boy's Stable	**8** Covered Arena	**13** Arena
3 Triangular Meeting Point	**6** North End of 40 Stall Barn	**9** School Pens	**14** Round Pen
		10 Race Track	**15** Parking
		11 Outdoor Round Pen	**Restrooms**

FLAG IS UP FARMS · 901 E. HWY 246 SOLVANG CA 93463

FLAG IS UP FARMS 1-805-688-4382 · LEARNING CENTER 1-805-688-3483
1-888-826-6689 · WWW.MONTYROBERTS.COM

A Monty Roberts Tutorial

To get a better understanding of Monty's discoveries and familiarize you with his distinct body of work, we have included several links.

ABOUT JOIN-UP

Monty Roberts first developed Join-Up to stop the cycle of violence typically used in traditional horse breaking. Through a process of clear communication and mutual trust, horses are motivated to be willing partners as they accept the first saddle, bridle, and rider of their lives in less than thirty minutes.

Watch a Join-Up on YouTube: "Monty Roberts Join Up Example"
(http://www.montyroberts.com/contacts/videos/).

MONTY DEMONSTRATES HIS APPROACH TO LOADING A HORSE ON A TRAILER

Calming a nervous horse is difficult, but as Monty demonstrates, it takes patience, collaboration, and mutual trust to accomplish the task.

Watch Monty load a horse on a horse trailer on YouTube: "Monty Roberts Horse Trailer Loading"
(http://www.montyroberts.com/contacts/videos/).

WATCH MONTY ON THE LONDON STAGE OF *WAR HORSE*

Watch Monty as he works to improve and authenticate the actors playing the horse onstage for War Horse on the London stage.

Watch Monty onstage at War Horse on YouTube: "Experiencing War Horse with Monty Roberts"
(http://www.montyroberts.com/contacts/videos/).

AN INTERESTING CONVERSATION WITH MONTY AND BRITISH ACTOR MARTIN CLUNES

Martin Clunes is one of England's most beloved actors. Martin and Monty share their passion for horses in this interesting conversation.

Watch Monty and Martin Clunes on YouTube: "Martin Clunes and Monty Roberts discuss Horsepower…"
(http://www.montyroberts.com/contacts/videos/).

Watch Monty and Martin Clunes complete a Join-Up on YouTube: "Martin Clunes-Horsepower: part 3"
(http://www.montyroberts.com/contacts/videos/).

LEARN ABOUT SHY BOY: THE MUSTANG WHO CAME IN FROM THE WILD

Shy Boy is the Mustang Monty adopted and still lives at Flag Is Up Farms.

Watch Monty and Shy Boy on YouTube: ""Shy Boy" Monty Roberts Part One"
(http://www.montyroberts.com/contacts/videos/).

WATCH MONTY AND HER MAJESTY QUEEN ELIZABETH II PRESENT THE ANIMAL ADVOCACY AWARD

On June 24, 2012, Her Majesty Queen Elizabeth II, Patron of Join-Up International, and Monty presented chosen recipients with awards for commitment to Monty's violence-free concepts. The Queen awarded signed certificates to acknowledge these individuals for their extraordinary efforts to eliminate violence in the training of horses. The ceremony took place during the Al Habtoor Royal Windsor Polo Cup, Guards Polo Club, Windsor, England.

Watch Monty Discuss the Animal Advocacy Award on YouTube: "Monty and Queen Elizabeth II Animal Advocacy Awards"
(http://www.montyroberts.com/contacts/videos/)

HORSE SENSE FOR SOLDIERS

Over the course of various clinics, Monty and his team have been working with veterans suffering from Post-Traumatic Stress Disorder (PTSD). These clinics help soldiers reconnect with hope, trust, and self-affirmation.

Watch how Join-Up Impacts soldiers suffering from PTSD: "Monty Roberts' Horse Sense and Soldiers Clinics"
(http://www.montyroberts.com/contacts/videos/)

About the Authors

Susan Cain, Ed.D., LCSW, is a business consultant and coach, mother and life-long equestrian. She is a partner with Dr. Tim Buividas at the Corporate Learning Institute, an established consultancy based in Chicago, Illinois. She serves as adjunct faculty at several Chicago area business schools. Susan's practice includes an international base of clientele. The Corporate Learning Institute provides custom-designed training solutions, strategic planning and performance coaching solutions. Learn more about Susan at http://us.linkedin.com/pub/dir/Susan/Cain.

Debbie Roberts-Loucks joined MPRI in 2002 to build Monty Robert's international training schedule and oversee MPRI's publishing, product development, and licensing. A graduate of UCLA, Debbie has extensive experience in sales, marketing, and new business development. Debbie's extensive background with horses, as well as her commitment to advance Monty's concepts, uniquely qualifies her to extend the MPRI brand into a global leadership organization impacting millions of individuals, companies, organizations, governments, and industries. Learn more about Debbie at http://www.linkedin.com/in/debbieloucks.

Find out more about Monty Roberts at www.montyroberts.com.

Appendix

Key Take-Aways by Chapter

Lesson 1: Value Your Purpose

- Knowing and valuing your strengths can act as a shield against self-doubt.

- Taking risks leads to increased learning.

- Awareness and appreciation of your own unique strengths and values can help you rebound from disappointments.

- It is easy to give up when others do not affirm you. Persistence takes courage and a deeper belief in your purpose and vision.

Lesson 2: Adversity - The Launch Pad For Personal Inspiration And Innovation

- Adversity is important for shaping potential as well as compassion.

- Many leaders report that adversity has helped them develop effective life and leadership skills.

- Resilience is an important protectant against stress in your life. Since research shows that resilience is learned, you too can improve your resilience levels.

- Key relationships help fuel self-worth and serve as a protectant support factor.

Lesson 3: Rebounding From Personal Adversity Using Communication & Risk

- Setbacks create learning opportunities that are cleverly disguised opportunities for personal growth.

- Standing up for yourself and stating your true feelings through confident communication is more useful than avoiding, backing down, or attacking others.

- Taking risks is uncomfortable, but it is the only way to grow, learn, and achieve your goals.

Lesson 4: Why Values Matter

- Values are the basis for many of your decisions, and make your approach unique.

- Knowing your values allows you to align your actions around what is important.

Lesson 5: Acceptance - A Useful Coping Tool

- Acceptance is a process.

- Trying to change the "unchangeables" in life will drain your energy.

- Accepting "unchangeables" will free up energy to be used elsewhere.

Lesson 6: Vulnerability - The Gateway To Compassion

- Vulnerability is shared by all living things.

- We often protect our vulnerability in ways that are not useful to us.

- Violence is never an effective means to meet the needs of a vulnerable person or animal.

Lesson 7: Affirmation - The Fuel That Builds Self-Worth

- In *How Full Is Your Bucket*, Tom Rath explains that we all have an "emotional bucket" that others can "dip" or "replace" from.

- When others "dip" or "replace" from our bucket, we feel emotionally depleted or charged.

- Affirmation, validation, and recognition build and stabilize self-worth.

- Self -affirmation is an important component of self-worth

Lesson 8: Putting It All Together

- Knowing your pivotal events can inform you about what experiences you had in your life that developed you into the person you are today.

- Monty's ability to learn from failure led him to invent the "Monty Roberts Blanket" for horses.

- Think about how you can apply your key learning's to your life.

References and Suggestions for Further Reading

Block, Peter. *Community; the Structure of Belonging.* Berrett-Koehler Publishers, 2009.

Brown, Brene. Daring Greatly: *How the Courage to Be Vulnerable Transforms the Way We Live, Love, Parent, and Lead.* Gotham, 2012.

Clifton, D.O., & Hodges, T.D. (in press). Strengths. In J.M. Burns (Ed.), *The Encyclopedia of Leadership.* Thousand Oaks, CA: Sage.

Haller, Howard Edward. *Adversity and Obstacles in the Shaping of prominent leaders; A Hermeneutic Phenomenological Inquiry.* The Leadership Success Institute and

Gonzaga University Doctoral Dissertation in Leadership Studies, 2008.

Haque, Umami. *The New Capitalist Manifesto: Building a Disruptively Better Business.* Harvard Business Review Press, 2010.

Pink, Dan. *Drive: The Surprising Truth about What Motivates Us.* Riverhead Books, 2011.

Rath, Tom. *How Full is Your Bucket? Positive Strategies for Work and Life.* Gallup Press, 2004.

Roberts, Monty. *The Man who Listens to Horses, The Story of a Real-Life Horse Whisperer.* Random House Digital, 2008.

Scott, Susan. *Fierce Conversations: Achieving Success at Work and in Life One Conversation at a Time.* Berkeley Trade, 2004.

Other Books by Monty Roberts

- Roberts, Monty. The Man Who Listens to Horses. Random House, August 1997, hardcover, 310 pages. ISBN 0-345-42705-X.

- Roberts, Monty. *The Man Who Listens to Horses* - abridged audio book. Random House Audio, August 1997. ISBN 978-0-679-46044-2.

- Roberts, Monty. *Shy Boy, the Horse that Came in from the Wild.* 1999, 239 pages. ISBN 0-676-97273-X

- Roberts, Monty. *Horse Sense for People: The Man Who Listens to Horses Talks to People.* 2002, 256 pages. ISBN 0-670-89975-5

- Roberts, Monty. *From My Hands to Yours: Lessons from a Lifetime of Training Championship Horses.* 2002, 230 pages. ISBN 1929256566

- Roberts, Monty. *The Horses in My Life.* 2002, 256 pages. ISBN 0755313453

- Roberts, Monty. *Ask Monty: Over 170 Most Common Horse Problems Solved.* 2009, 320 pages. ISBN 0755317238

- Roberts, Monty. *I'm Shy Boy: Here's My Story.* Solvang, CA: M. and P. Roberts, 2010. Print. ISBN 978-1-929256-61-7

- Roberts, Monty. *The Little American Mustang.* Solvang, CA: Monty and Pat Roberts, 2010. Print.

Image Credits

Lesson 1: Courtesy Monty and Pat Roberts, Inc. Archives

Wild Mustangs: Debbie Roberts-Loucks 2011

Lesson 2: Courtesy Monty and Pat Roberts, Inc. Archives

Monty on Ginger: Courtesy Monty and Pat Roberts, Inc. Archives

Lesson 3: Courtesy Monty and Pat Roberts, Inc. Archives

Monty completing a successful Join-Up: Courtesy Monty and Pat Roberts, Inc. Archives

Monty signing copies: Courtesy Monty and Pat Roberts, Inc. Archives

Lesson 4: Daniel J. Quinajon

Entrance to Flag: Courtesy Monty and Pat Roberts, Inc. Archives

Lesson 5: Theta-Sigma

Monty and Shy with students: Courtesy Monty and Pat Roberts, Inc. Archives

Lesson 6: Courtesy Monty and Pat Roberts, Inc. Archives

Monty practicing: Courtesy Monty and Pat Roberts, Inc. Archives

Lesson 7: Simon Palmer Into-the-Lens

With Queen: Simon Palmer Into-the-Lens

Lesson 8: Courtesy Monty and Pat Roberts, Inc. Archives

Same photo: Courtesy Monty and Pat Roberts, Inc. Archives (The first saddle of this horse's life.)

Write the Next Chapter of Your Life

This eBook is available in a printed format and the *Life Lessons From The Man Who Listens To Horses* workshop can be offered at any location in the world.

What you will Learn...

- Tools to increase self-awareness and personal value.

- New techniques to rebound from setbacks and build resilience.

- A take-away action plan to think about the possibilities in your life.

Program Overview

The workshop is designed to optimize learning within a compact period of time. The session is fast-paced, active and inspirational.

Lesson 1: Value Your Purpose

Lesson 2: Adversity– The Launch Pad for Personal Inspiration and Innovation

Lesson 3: Rebounding from Setbacks

Lesson 4: Why Values Matter

Lesson 5: Acceptance– A Useful Coping Tool

Lesson 6: Vulnerability– The Gateway to Compassion

Participants will be inspired by Monty Robert's life journey and apply lessons to their own lives. Contact us below to hold a session anywhere in the world.

Find us on Amazon.com
Contact Susan Cain at
scain@corplearning.com

Visit our Facebook Page at
https://www.facebook.com/LifeLessonsFromTheManWhoLis
tensToHorses?ref=hl

Made in the USA
San Bernardino, CA
23 February 2017